the true book of

METRIC MEASUREMENT

by June Behrens

illustrated by Tom Dunnington

CHILDRENS PRESS, CHICAGO

*The author wishes to thank
Pat Oberg, Math Consultant
for the Manhattan Beach Schools,
for her assistance in the preparation
of this manuscript.*

Library of Congress Cataloging in Publication Data

Behrens, June
   The true book of metric measurement.

   SUMMARY: An easy-to-read history of the metric system and explanation of its different units.
   1. Metric system—Juvenile literature. [1. Metric
system] I. Dunnington, Tom, ill. II. Title.
QC92.5.B43   389'.152   74-23231
ISBN 0-516-01146-4

7 8 9 10 11 12 R 78

A long time ago people used parts of their bodies to measure things.

They used their foot or hand or finger.

Sometimes they measured in steps to see how long something was.

Different people were different
sizes.

A big farmer measured his field in
giant steps.

A little farmer measured his field
in small steps.

When they stepped off their fields, the numbers of steps were different for each farmer.

Even though the fields were the same size, the farmers did not get the same numbers.

Do you know why?

In England, the kings wanted their people to have one way of measuring.

They made measures in feet and yards.

The feet and yards measured how long something was.

Then everyone got the same numbers when they measured the same things.

When the colonists came to America, they brought the English way of measuring with them.

Later, the colonies united to become the United States.

Most of their trade was with England.

Trade was easier when both countries used the same measurement.

Some people in France thought of another way to measure.

They would not use feet and yards.

They would use a part of the distance around the earth as a way to measure.

The measurement invented by the Frenchmen was the meter.

All other ways they measured length would be based on the meter.

The French way to measure was very easy.

Each measurement could be
made larger or smaller by
multiplying or dividing by 10.

The French called their new way of measuring the metric system.

Tools to measure were made.

Now everyone could measure with these tools and get the same numbers.

The scientists of many nations liked the French measurement.

The metric system became the language of scientists all over the world.

Over one hundred years ago leaders in the United States made a law.

The law said that people could use the metric system of measurement.

But people liked the old way of using feet and inches and yards.

They did not change.

Today, all but a few countries use metric measurement.

Someday, all the countries of the world may use the metric system.

Nations and people can work better together when they know and use the same number language.

COUNTRIES USING OR NOW CONVERTING TO
METRIC MEASUREMENT

COUNTRIES NOT USING METRIC MEASUREMENT

METER

We measure in meters when we want to know how long something is.

A meter is about as long as a softball bat.

Three of your father's footprints in a row are about a meter long.

When we want to measure the
length of the bike rack we use
meters.

We measure our bed, the size of
our room, or around our yard in
meters.

When we measure, there is a short way of writing meter.
We use the letter **m** for meter.

Let's measure.
Take a yardstick and add the width of your hand to it.
Cut a string that long.
The string will be about a meter long.

Use your string.

Measure the teacher's desk.

How wide is the classroom door?

How far can you reach? Is that
about a meter?

Is the lunch bench more or less than two meters long?

Use the string to measure other things in your classroom.

CENTIMETER

Did you find some things that were not as long as a meter?

When we want to measure something **less than** a meter, we add centi to meter.

We use centimeters to measure ladybugs and lizards, pencils and books.

A centimeter is this __ long.

A paper clip is about 1 centimeter wide.

Look at your ruler.
Count the centimeters on your ruler.

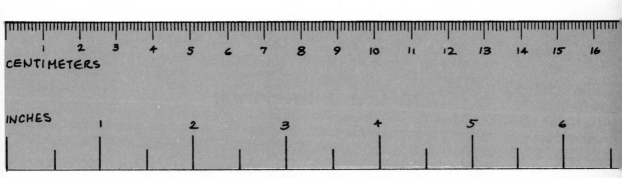

There are 100 centimeters in one meter.

This is the same number as pennies in a dollar.

Using your ruler, you can make a string exactly 100 centimeters, or 1 meter long.

The short way of writing
centimeter is **cm.**

Let's measure.

Use the centimeters marked on
your ruler.

Measure your pencil.

How long is your foot?

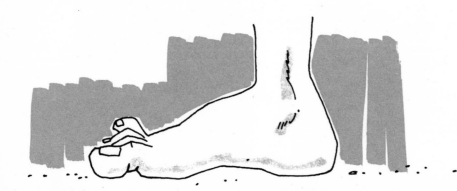

How wide is your finger?

If you measure 110 centimeters, are you more or less than a meter tall?

Would it take a long time to measure the distance from your house to school?

When we measure long distances, we add meters together.

We add the word kilo to meter.

KILOMETER

There are 1000 meters in one kilometer.

The short way to write kilometer is **km.**

We use kilometers to measure the distance to school, to another town or across the country.

GRAM

We measure in grams when we want to know how much something weighs.

Something very light weighs a gram.

A bean weighs about a gram.

A safety pin, one peanut and a
paper clip weigh about a gram
each.

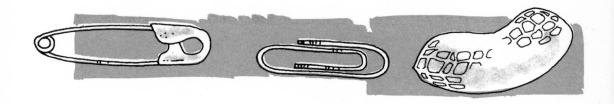

A penny weighs about three
grams.

A big, new crayon weighs about
ten grams.

A walnut is heavy.

It might weigh about 28 grams.

When we want to weigh a nail, a marshmallow or a piece of fruit, we find out how many grams it weighs.

There is a short way of writing grams.

We use the letter **g** for grams.

Sometimes we use a balance scale.

On a balance scale we can see when something is more than, less than or just the same weight.

Look on a can of food.

Does it tell how many grams the food inside weighs?

KILOGRAM

When we weigh something heavier, we add grams together.

We add the word kilo to gram.

There are 1000 grams in one kilogram.

When we weigh something heavy, like ourselves, a big sack of potatoes or a turkey we weigh in kilograms.

A short way to write kilogram is **kg.**
Do you have a big dog?
If he is really big, he will weigh
about 20 kilograms.

A fat pumpkin might weigh about 5 kilograms.

Will your bicycle weigh more or less than 10 kilograms?

MEGAGRAM

When we weigh something VERY
big and heavy, we add kilograms
together to get a megagram.

A truck or a whale might weigh
more than a megagram.

A megagram is one million grams.

LITER

Liquids, or things you can pour, are measured in liters.

A glass of orange juice or milk is measured in liters.

Water and pop are measured in liters.

One liter is about four tall glasses of milk.

It takes four cartons of orange juice to make about a liter.

A liter is about 2½ cans of pop. You wouldn't drink a liter all at one time!

The car might use many liters of gas to get to the next town.

Father may need 80 liters to fill the gas tank.

The short way of writing liter is **l.**

MILLILITER

When we measure an amount less than a liter, we add milli to liter.

We use milliliters to measure a drop of water, a teaspoon of medicine or a cup of milk.

There are 1000 milliliters in one liter.

The short way of writing milliliter is **ml.**

There are five milliliters in one teaspoonful.

Father's cup of coffee will measure about 230 milliliters.

One can of pop is about 400 milliliters.

Would we measure a big raindrop in liters or milliliters?

CELSIUS SCALE

We measure temperature on the Celsius scale.

This scale, or thermometer, tells us how hot or cold something is.

We call the scale Celsius after the man who invented it.

The Celsius thermometer is sometimes called the centigrade thermometer.

A short way of writing Celsius is **C.**

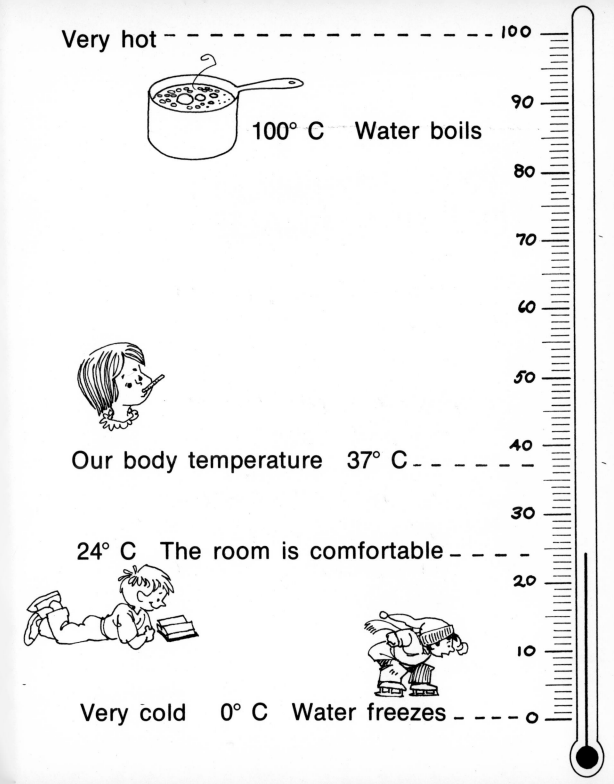

Very hot - - - - - - - - - - - - 100

100° C   Water boils

90

80

70

60

50

Our body temperature   37° C - - - - - - 40

30

24° C   The room is comfortable - - - -

20

10

Very cold   0° C   Water freezes - - - - 0

THE SHORT WAY

OF WRITING

METRIC MEASUREMENTS

When we measure length
  m is for meter
  cm is for centimeter
  cm is less than a meter
  km is for kilometer
  km is more than a meter

When we measure weight
  g is for gram
  mg is for milligram
  mg is less than a gram
  kg is for kilogram
  kg is more than a gram

When we measure liquid
  l is for liter
  cl is for centiliter
  cl is less than a liter
  ml is for milliliter
  ml is less than a centiliter

When we measure temperature
  C is for Celsius or centigrade

APPROXIMATE CONVERSIONS
FROM METRIC MEASURES

SYMBOL	WHEN YOU KNOW	MULTIPLY BY	TO FIND	SYMBOL
		LENGTH		
mm	millimeters	0.04	inches	in
cm	centimeters	0.4	inches	in
m	meters	3.3	feet	ft
m	meters	1.1	yards	yd
km	kilometers	0.6	miles	mi
		WEIGHT		
g	grams	0.035	ounces	oz
kg	kilograms	2.2	pounds	lb
		VOLUME		
ml	milliliters	0.03	fluid ounces	fl oz
l	liters	2.1	pints	pt
l	liters	1.06	quarts	qt
l	liters	0.26	gallons	gal
		TEMPERATURE		
°C	Celsius temperature	9/5 (then add 32)	Fahrenheit temperature	°F